Then & Now

MEDWAY TOWNS

Rochester from the bridge. This postcard is dated 1905 but the picture shows the old tower of Rochester Cathedral before it was replaced by the current spire in 1904. Although the tide is low, a huffler has been employed to help the two-man crew of the Rochester sailing barge to lower the mast and sail in order to shoot Rochester bridge. He is working the windlass in the bow, having rowed from the pier on the far bank of the Medway (the Rochester side); his own boat is tied to the stern. Sailing barges such as this were the most numerous form of local transport. Thousands were registered in Rochester alone in the late nineteenth century.

Then & Now

MEDWAY TOWNS

COMPILED BY ALUN PEDLER

TEMPUS

First published 1999
Copyright © Alun Pedler, 1999

Tempus Publishing Limited
The Mill, Brimscombe Port,
Stroud, Gloucestershire, GL5 2QG

ISBN 0 7524 1623 5

Typesetting and origination by
Tempus Publishing Limited
Printed in Great Britain by
Midway Clark Printing, Wiltshire

Chatham. Town Hall and Club

This view of 1906 shows Chatham Town Hall which was built between 1898 and 1900. Behind the Town Hall is the Sailors' Home and to the left is the Paddock. At the end of Military Road, to the right, is the Eagle Tavern and the building next door with the balconies is the Chatham Constitutional Club, opened in 1899 for gentlemen's leisure with billiard, smoking and reading rooms. The open-top tram advertises Fry's Cocoa.

CONTENTS

This postcard of 1915 shows Gillingham High Street looking east, close to Marlborough Road. On the left are general stores and butchers.

On the right nearest the camera is the Lord (now Viscount) Hardinge public house, dating from 1850. Called the Lord Hardinge from 1900 until 1939 but the Viscount before and after, in 1909 it was the only public house in Gillingham allowed to open for weekday hours on Christmas Day if it fell during the week – all other pubs had to abide by Sunday hours. Beyond that is the Invicta cinema owned by H.G. and W. Croneen, who owned a number of other cinemas in the Medway area. It was opened on Easter Monday 1914 and closed in July 1931, with a brief renaissance as the Coliseum Theatre until 1932. Beyond the Invicta are the shops of J. Oliver (tobacconist) and Robert Blagdon (fruiterer).

ACKNOWLEDGEMENTS

This book has been created in partnership with the Medway Archives and Local Studies Centre and a huge debt of gratitude is owed to the staff, especially Norma Crowe, for many of the 'then' photographs. Similarly, grateful thanks to Dudley Studios, Mr O. Wenborn and Lucas Varity for making photographs freely available. Others appear by kind permission of the Guildhall Museum.

For their time, information and access for the new photographs thanks are due to the public, householders and shopkeepers of the Towns. Special thanks are due to John Hetterley of Lucas Varity, PC Roscoe Walford, Mr Goldsmith (Best Street), Justine Pannett and Peter McKenna (Medway Hospital), Ernie Mackay (Medway Velo CC), Wingets Tennis Club, Kent County Council Arts and Libraries and especially Rob Stead and the lads of Cliffe Fire Service for giving up their spare time. As the great British summer of 1998 defeated my attempts to complete the new pictures, thanks must be given to my 'oldest' friend Alan Williams for taking the better quality new photographs.

Why a Medway book from a North Wales man? Because I was brought up in Strood, where my parents and sister plus family still live, so thanks to them for putting me up (or putting up with me) these many years. Finally for the book production itself, thanks to Thelma Hinds for wordsmithing, the Golden Idea for graphic layout advice and Alex Cameron at Tempus.

INTRODUCTION

The Medway Towns is a term given essentially to the area of Strood, Rochester, Chatham and Gillingham stretching from west to east on the River Medway in Kent. It also contains areas that were once free-standing villages, like Frindsbury, Borstal, Brompton and Rainham, but which are now, to the uninitiated, indistinguishably merged into the larger conurbations. There are also a few villages that are still separate, for the purposes of this book at least, like Upnor and Higham. The key link, though, is the river itself to which the Medway Towns owe their growth. The area was first settled in about 2000 BC by hunters, farmers and fishermen on what was then considerable marshland overlooked by chalk hills. By the first century BC they were succeeded by the Belgae tribe from Europe, also a farming community. A major expansion took place after the area was captured in the Roman advance of AD 43, when what is now Rochester became an important town – Durobrivae – at the point where Watling Street bridges the Medway. Here the town was strengthened and protected by earthworks and later city walls, with the previously wooden buildings replaced by brick and stone, and the first permanent bridge was built. The departure of the Romans was followed by a succession of invasions and settlements by warring tribes, notably Jutes, Danes and Mercians, although sufficient stability allowed the construction of a cathedral in 604. The next period of expansion came after the Norman Conquest which saw the building of the castle (started in 1088) and cathedral (started 1080), as well as renovation and strengthening of the previous Roman city wall. The *Domesday Book* refers at this time to Strood (then a part of Frindsbury), Chatham and Gillingham, albeit as minor villages. St Bartholomew's Hospital was also founded around the same time. The Middle Ages saw continuous expansion and prosperity with considerable trading in fish, farm produce, iron and paper. A new bridge of stone had been constructed in 1392 and there was another slow but sure expansion of population causing the scattered settlements to merge closer together, still dominated by Rochester. Much of the surrounding area remained as farmland.

New growth both in population and the Medway Towns' fortunes was caused by the creation of Chatham Dockyard by Elizabeth I in 1570. Not only did this attract more workers and subsequent housing needs, but also an upsurge in ancillary services and the creation of barracks for Royal Navy, Royal Engineers and Royal Marines personnel. Large areas of Chatham, Brompton (then a separate entity) and Gillingham were given over to residential housing through the eighteenth and nineteenth centuries. New roads were built and two railway bridges over the Medway, erected by competing companies, opened up rail travel to London.

Most of the goods were carried by road or river: raw materials, including much timber, came into the Towns from the Baltic for the Dockyard and other construction works and completed goods such as cement and bricks were exported in the ubiquitous Medway barges of which 1,000 were registered in Rochester alone at the end of the nineteenth century. By this time the Medway Towns were a thriving, bustling cosmopolitan city with numerous shopping areas and a diverse industrial region, although still centred around the needs of the armed forces.

Charles Dickens had put Rochester on the map, the Dockyard had done the same for Chatham. Trams arrived in 1902, opening up cheap transport throughout the Towns. Entertainment was provided by numerous variety theatres (later cinemas), public houses, swimming baths and the various sports, clubs and societies. A number of excellent educational establishments have existed since the re-founding of the King's School, Rochester, by King Henry VIII in 1542. Parks and open spaces such as Victoria Gardens,

A very early (*c.* 1860) view of Brompton High Street, showing Arlidge, cabinet makers and undertakers, on the near right. Close by is the Golden Lion public house – one of the oldest surviving inns in Gillingham. As can be seen, deliveries to and from the local shops were mostly by handcarts or larger horse-drawn carts.

Castle Gardens, the Vines and numerous local recreational grounds were laid out, mostly by the local corporations for the use and well-being of the general public. The relative prosperity and generally pleasant way of life in the Towns attracted an ever-increasing population which resulted in a surge of residential buildings. This boom began in Waldeslade, Wigmore and Hempstead in the 1930s but reached a peak in the 1950s and 1960s which saw most of the gaps in the Towns filled in by housing, mostly to the south. The Medway Towns now stretch from the outskirts of rural Strood to the estates of Wigmore, containing a rich diversity of town and country, industry and commerce, road and rail, with examples of the old meeting sometime incongruously with the ultra-modern.

This book therefore attempts to show a flavour of both the old, represented by photographs and postcards ranging from 1880 to 1940 (mainly from the period 1902 to 1912), and the new, the majority taken in 1998 from the exact same vantage point. It covers both the commonplace and the more unusual, commercial and residential and is intended to reflect the change across a diverse area. In addition there are sections dedicated to the working day and leisure pursuits that show how the nature of these two aspects have changed (or not) during this century.

Even this can only be a snapshot in time as change is constant in the Towns; witness the closure of the Dockyard and much heavy industry in recent years to be replaced by consumerism and the growth of the heritage industry. Much of the change has been necessary, perhaps, to improve transport and communication links and it can be argued that the advent of the motor car has been the single greatest impact on the fabric of the Towns. This has served, paradoxically, both to increase diversification and help merge the disparate Towns into one.

St Nicholas' church and Strood High Street at six o'clock on a summer's evening in the 1920s. The awning on the left is shading the premises of Miss A.E. Edmonds, fancy draper. Beyond the church are the works of Budden and Biggs, local brewers. On the right the shops are Arthrell's (fruiterer), Cason (grocer), Miss Ellen Terry (confectioner), John Terry (butcher), then the Unemployment Insurance office, the Tax Collector and Lucas the bootmaker.

Chapter 1

STROOD AND THE VILLAGES

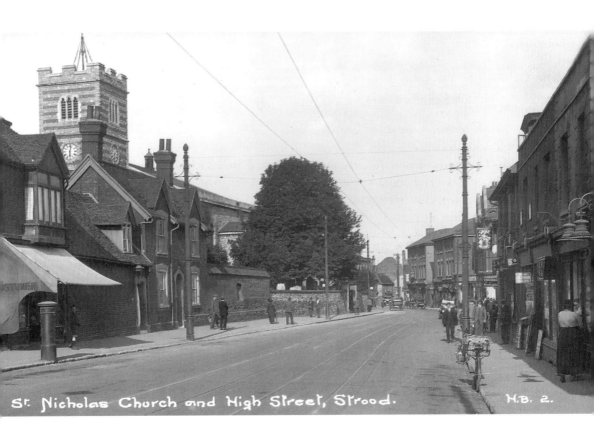

St. Nicholas Church and High Street, Strood.   H.B. 2.

This 1907 postcard shows the imposing St Nicholas' vicarage which stood between the south end of Montfort Road and Strood Hill, behind St Nicholas' infants' and girls' school. The vicar at the time was Walter James Tait MA, former fellow and tutor at Worcester College, Oxford. In the latter years of the nineteenth century the vicarage had a net income of £79 with two acres of glebe (land assigned to a clergyman) and residence. It ceased to be a vicarage in the 1960s and was taken over by Kent County Council's Strood Youth Centre Club in the 1970s. The upkeep became too costly, though, and the building was pulled down in 1994. The new building was opened on August 1995 and offers sports, drama activities and open evenings for clubs etc.

St Nicholas' School stood opposite St Nicholas' church on the corner of Commercial Road and is seen here in the early 1900s. Kelly's Directory stated that it was completed in 1885; other sources state 1871. The original school had been built on Strood Hill in 1849 and by 1900 housed only infants and primary girls (190 of each). The school shown here had housed primary boys only (240) since 1875. Next door is Wiles and Robinson (carriage builders), then John Elvy (coal merchant), Skinner Bros (farriers), Ernest Carter (watchmaker), Ernest Baron (hairdresser) and the Rochester, Chatham and District Laundry. Now Commercial Road has widened and the corner is taken up by Spikegeneral Car

Sales before a small parade of shops which apart from Digby's pine furniture store are all estate agents.

The High Street, looking towards the Angel. On the left is thought to be the Red Lion and Star public house, an ancient building with massive oak beams and a carved ceiling. It was originally the Ferry House, as a creek of the Medway flowed to within a few yards opposite. At the time of the photograph in the very early years of this century the landlord was Stephen Rowing but the pub disappeared by 1904 and the licence was moved to the Cecil Arms. Next door is Leonard Dale's grocers, opposite and facing the junction is the original Angel Inn and next door to that the premises of Henry Palmer, saddler, and F.W. Palmer, cabinet maker. Today the High Street has been widened and the North Street junction has been enlarged, with the shops moved back from the road.

The 1909 postcard of the High Street looking east shows the Angel Inn on the left then the Palmer establishments (see p. 12). Next are Thomas Colling's ironmongers, W. and R. Fletcher's butchers, a gap for Newark Yard and the gable end of the London Provincial Bank. Opposite with the three golden balls is Smetham and Tutt, pawnbrokers, Pierson's newsagents, with Ostler and Green, chemists, next door. Today all the original east side has been swept away and taken back for shops and a pedestrian area before Barclays Bank. The High Street itself has been considerably widened to ease traffic flow.

The view to the west, dated 1908, shows the Angel Inn in the centre. Immediately to the left of the photograph is the post office, then run by Albert Hudson and containing the Stanmore Press and Public Call Office. Next, at 77-81 are Cobb & Son, drapers, outfitters and house furnishers, then Percy Jordan's dairy (Jordan also owned a grocer's shop at no. 82 opposite, next to the Fountain public house). It is probable that the cart belongs to the firm as the sign on the back seems to read Fruiterer and Dairy. Nowadays the effects of road widening are obvious and the shops have changed to clothes outlets, estate agents, Boots and the Co-op on the left, and Starburgers, dry cleaners and opticians on the right. Further along is Paulley's fishmongers who have been in the High Street since 1928, the longest-serving shop apart from Fernbanks (see p. 15).

Fernbank's jewellers have been in the Medway Towns for over a hundred years, founded by two Austrian brothers named Fehrenbach in 1880. They originally traded from the back of a cart before opening shops at 54 High Street, Chatham, and in Strood where the clock (seen in both photographs) has been a landmark for over a century and is still mostly original. The shop used to sell more domestic goods, such as canteens of cutlery, as well as watches and jewellery. In the early years of the century, the adjoining property (no. 63, Carter Owen & Co., wine merchants) was demolished, opening up a gap leading to Pelican Wharf and Medway Cottages – which later became part of Strood's one-way system, called Commercial Road. Since then, Fernbank's has remained the corner property.

The name was changed to Fernbank before the Second World War, during which the firm was sub-contracted by Short Bros, the aircraft manufacturers in Rochester, to produce precisely engineered parts and clocks. They were praised for their war effort by the Ministry of Production, especially for their high standards of efficiency and precise methods adopted in training female staff. The firm passed out of family hands in the late 1980s but the tradition of fine quality is carried on by the present owner Anita Bishop, shown in the doorway.

STROOD. S.E.R. STATION. SEPT 1854

The South Eastern Railway opened up the North Kent line to London from Strood in 1845 using the former canal tunnel to Higham. The Strood rail terminus was then nearer to Canal Road. Although the postcard is dated September 1854, official records show the new station was opened in June 1856. The waterway in the foreground, possibly feeding a tidal millpond alongside and under Canal Road, was filled in to allow New Road, later renamed Station Road, to be built. Behind the camera was marshland and orchards up to Frindsbury Road. The station was rebuilt and extended to cater for increased traffic in 1866 and the current building dates from 1973. In the new picture a train is shown on the line to Maidstone; the more heavily utilized commuter lines to Charing Cross and Cannon Street are beyond.

The late nineteenth century saw considerable railway competition. The South Eastern Railway linked Strood to London in 1849 and later the London, Chatham and Dover Railway (formerly East Kent) linked East Kent to Chatham by 1858. Line-sharing arrangements could not be agreed so the LCDR built its own railway bridge across the Medway and opened up a line to London Victoria in 1860. This included the building of a viaduct and Rochester Bridge station, which itself was rebuilt in 1908 as shown on this poscard of 1914. The SER had built a second railway bridge in 1892. Competition ceased in 1899 when the companies merged to form the South Eastern and Chatham Railway, making one bridge redundant. Rochester Bridge station closed on 1 January 1917 as a

wartime economy measure and was finally demolished, with great difficulty because of the solid Yorkshire stone used in its construction, in 1968 to allow road widening and conversion of the bridge from rail to road traffic. The site is now part of Passmore's yard.

Strood Docks owed their origins to the Thames and Medway Canal which was built to connect the two rivers via tunnels through the chalk between Strood and Higham. It saved a fifty-mile sail around the North Kent coast and protected ships from attacks by the French. The canal was opened on

4 October 1824, the tunnel being at that time the largest in Britain. It was greatly welcomed by the Royal Navy. Strood Docks were built to take the ships of up to 300, later 600, tons and a pump was installed to maintain water levels in the canal. The tunnel was converted to rail use in 1845 and the docks were bought by the railway company, which installed sidings, cattle pens, stables, cranes and goods sheds. Considerable trade in timber and cement passed through and the picture taken at the turn of the century shows the loading and unloading of at least five ships. Victoria Wharf, which later burnt down in 1916, can also be seen. The docks closed in 1963 and were filled in in 1987. Now there are builders' merchants on most of the site, the remainder being a residential estate built in 1997 and still expanding, called Mariners' Way.

The area between the railway bridge carrying the Strood-Maidstone line (right) and Zoar Chapel (left) in the early 1900s. Zoar Chapel was the oldest place of worship in Strood. It was built by Protestant Dissenters of the Independent Denomination in 1786. It could hold a congregation of 300 and had a small burial ground at the rear which as consecrated ground caused legal problems when the demolition of the building was proposed. At no. 35 is Edward Palmer, gunmaker and cutler, advertised as Sportsman's Supply Stores, at no. 37 Mrs George E. Evenden, basket, toy and fancy repository and next is the Old George public house, proprietor T. Rogers. Now, apart from the Medway Lounge Suites

and Bed Centre nestling by the bridge, the area is given over to the forecourt of a Repsol petrol station.

DICKENS' OLD PICKWICK. COBHAM. KENT.   59

The Leather Bottle public house, Cobham, in 1909, then with the addition of 'Dickens Old Pickwick' on the sign. Cobham (originally 'Cobba's ham' or boundary of Cobba's water meadow) dates from the twelfth century, the parish church of St Mary Magdalene from the early thirteenth, and much of the village from the eighteenth. Charles Dickens, a frequent visitor, put the village on the tourist trail by describing a visit to the Leather Bottle by Pickwick, Winkle and Snodgrass in *Pickwick Papers*. The inn was renovated and the nineteenth-century cladding was removed in the 1920s by Russel's Brewery and it still retains a considerable amount of Dickensian memorabilia. Cobham still has a timeless charm and appears, like other villages in the area, less touched by constant, intrusive traffic than the larger towns.

The name Higham now covers what were three separate locations: the original Lower Higham or Church Street, built around the church of St Mary the Virgin on reclaimed marshland; then the new Lower Higham clustered around the railway station; and Upper Higham, closer to the A2 trunk road and Gadshill Place, the erstwhile home of Charles Dickens. The postcard of 1910 shows the Railway Tavern and Chequers Inn in Lower Higham with the post office also to the left in Brookers Place. As can be seen, very little has changed apart from repainting, the loss of chimneys and the addition of a telephone box. Even the telegraph pole remains and the evidence of horses is replaced by that of horsepower.

Higham Village.

A view down Four Elms Hill (now A228) in Chattenden to Wainscott and Strood. The small track to the left led to Beacon Hill, where the beacon was originally used for signalling purposes. Later a small brickworks was built by George Hankey of the City of London and Beacon Hill was often used for picnics overlooking Upnor. Four Elms Hill itself could become impassable in bad weather and was known as Stickfast Hill. Just down the hill can be seen the girder of the military railway linking Chattenden Barracks, where ammunition was made at Lodge Hill, to the magazine at Upnor where it was loaded onto warships from Chatham Dockyard. Chattenden depot itself was built by convict labour and the railway line was completed in 1870. All has now been swept away to accommodate the widening of the major route to the Isle of Grain. Beacon Hill is now mostly MOD property and houses an archery club.

There are two Upnors: Lower along the river front and Upper, shown here in 1906. It consisted mainly of the one street with many houses in local weatherboarding, leading down to the River Medway and Upnor Castle which was built in 1567 to defend Chatham Dockyard opposite. (It failed dismally to do so in the Dutch raid of 1667.) The Upnor Castle public house on the left is now a private house, as is the shop which still sports the sign 'Stone Bros bakers and grocers' on the far gable end. The public house is the Kings Head which was bought from the brewery in 1972 and renamed the Tudor Rose. Note the surviving cobbled road surface.

Cliffe was an important centre in Saxon days and remained so in medieval times as it was much nearer the then shoreline. Decline set in, culminating in the fire which destroyed the timber-built town in 1520. The opening of the cement works in 1868 added to the expansion caused by the building of the Thames and Medway tunnel. The view of 1911 shows the High Street looking north with the weatherboarded H. Pope & Co. Supply Stores to the right, then the Victoria Inn public house. Further down and opposite were houses owned by the church used for those locals who had fallen on hard times. The scene is little changed today save for Pope's now being a listed building housing Wilkies restaurant.

This map of Rochester from around 1912 shows the major buildings of interest and prominent highways. Some unnamed roads have apparently been inserted for symmetry as they do not appear on contemporary Ordnance Survey maps, such as the mythical main road to Upnor from Strood Docks and streets off the High Street. The bridges are clearly shown as two for rail and one for road traffic.

Chapter 2

ROCHESTER

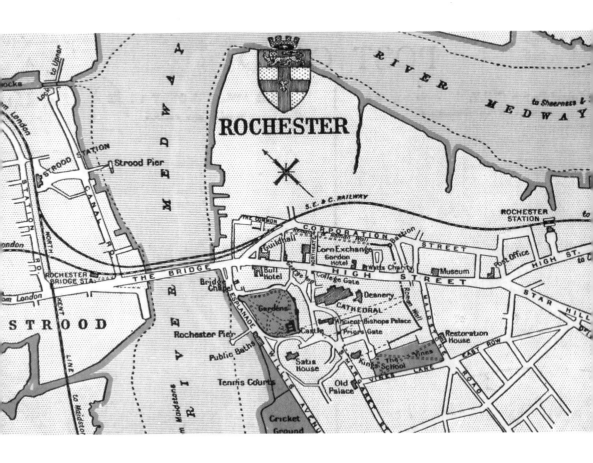

This unposted card is entitled 'The first Tram through Rochester', which dates it precisely to April 1908. Trams had first appeared on 17 June 1902 but were restricted to twenty-five Chatham and District Light Railway Company vehicles garaged at Luton,

covering routes from Luton to the Dockyard, Gillingham station and Pier Road. New lines were opened between 1904 and 1908, eventually through to Strood and then to Strood Hill or Frinsbury immediately after the special featured on the card. Trams lasted until 30 September 1930 when Leyland Titan buses took over. All trams were open-topped and restricted to a maximum speed of 16mph. On the left is the Gundulph public house, behind it the White Hart and opposite, the Crown Hotel. The Gundulph and all the properties beyond it as far as the White Hart (now called Expectations) were demolished when the railway bridge was converted to road use and the junction with Corporation Street widened between 1968 and 1970.

An early photograph from the castle shows the medieval road bridge (built between 1387 and 1392) and the replacement cast iron bridge necessary because of increased road and river traffic, completed in 1856 (later rebuilt in 1914). Demolition of the old bridge started in 1856 and required considerable explosive works by the Royal Engineers. The 1392 bridge had replaced an earlier wooden Saxon one constructed around 960 on the line of the present road bridge. It consisted of nine piers with ten arches each 43ft wide, the total length being 431ft with a width of 10ft. Each pier was allocated to a person or parish for upkeep: Rochester, the King, the Bishop of Rochester, the Archbishop of Canterbury, Hundred of Hoo etc. but they suffered from rotting, fire and damage. The stone replacement was

560ft long, 15ft wide and had eleven arches administered by the bridge wardens. The alignment of the old bridge was to the south of the present one, joining a point at the end of Strood Esplanade to Castle Hill. The stone balustrades were later used to enhance Rochester Esplanade from 1856. The white building in the centre of the Strood side was the Ship Inn.

The works of George Spinks, motor launch builder, on the Esplanade below the castle in 1915, seen from a landing stage in the river. The firm operated an extensive boatyard which built and repaired smaller boats as well.

To the left is the Medway Bathing Establishment, founded by local benefactor Richard Watts in 1880, containing first class, second class and plunge baths plus a swimming bath. It was built on the site of the Castle Club Old Baths and lasted until 1935 when an open-air swimming pool was built on the site of Spinks' boatyard. The white house to the right of the castle is Satis House, erstwhile home of Richard Watts. It received its name when Queen Elizabeth I, on being asked how she liked the house, replied 'Satis' – it is satisfactory. Today's picture shows the headquarters and car park of the Rochester Cruising Club on the site of Spinks.

Rochester Castle was built as a motte and bailey in 1085, but after a siege Bishop Gundulph commissioned William de Corbeil to build a stone castle which was completed in 1127. It was besieged again in 1215 by opponents of King John and in 1264 by Simon de Montfort, and suffered extensive damage. In the Middle Ages it fell into disrepair, passing via various marriages into the hands of the Earl of Jersey. At that time, in the mid-nineteenth century, the gardens were given over to allotments. It was leased to the Corporation in 1870 and later bought outright for £6,572 in 1884 with the object of laying out the grounds as public pleasure grounds. The bandstand had been constructed in 1871 and the terraces laid out slightly later. The bandstand has now gone, apart from the

plinth, as has much of the vegetation, removed for the staging of a historical pageant in 1931. The terrace itself has remained unaltered for a century, however, with its commanding views over the Medway and Esplanade.

Rochester Castle & New Terrace.

H.Bros.S.1002.

The old view shows the cathedral in 1902. It was originally built between 1080 and 1130, having been commissioned by Bishop Gundulph to replace the original built in 604 by St Justus, one of St Augustine's missionaries. A wooden tower and spire were added in 1343 but like the castle (see p. 29) had fallen into disrepair by the late nineteenth century, losing the spire in 1823. Much renovation then took place, funded by local benefactor Thomas Hellyar Foord, culminating in the restoration of the spire by 1904 as seen in the new photograph. The field in the foreground, St Mary's Meadow, was behind High Street shops that were pulled down in the late nineteenth century to open up the aspect and is now the site of the war memorial. The ornamental gateway at the rear was opened in 1958.

The postcard of 1904 shows Rochester High Street looking west, dominated as now by the Corn Exchange clock. The Corn Exchange was originally a butchers' market, then the Guildhall and became the Corn Exchange in 1698. The clock was donated in 1706 by Sir Cloudesley Shovell, Knight, Rear Admiral of the Blue and local MP, who also paid for renovation of the Exchange itself. From October 1910 the Corn Exchange became the first cinema in Rochester. Next door, nearer the camera, are the premises of Robson & Son, plumber, John Benjamin Frith, chemist, and George Kent, general stores (and also advertising at one time a Wonderful Mutoscope, admission free). These have been replaced by the Singapora Restaurant, a model toy shop and Dodgers Restaurant. On the left is the Kings Hotel, little changed today.

The Mathematical School was founded by Sir Joseph Williamson, MP for Rochester, by his will of 1701 which left £5,000 for the 'building and maintaining of a free school at Rochester, to educate the sons of freemen of the city towards the mathematics and other things that might encourage them to the sea service'. The building was erected in 1708 in the filled-up moat by the city wall and further rooms were added in 1840, 1882 and 1893, as shown on the card of 1905. School rooms stretched the length of Free School Lane to Corporation Street. The front door in the High Street was reserved for masters and prefects, while the lower orders used Free School Lane. The motto of the school, painted across the back of the hall, was 'Knowledge is a step which few may climb, but duty is a path which all may tread', which became the traditional punishment in writing lines. The building to the right was a confectioners, which became the school tuck shop. A new building was opened in the late 1950s in upper Maidstone Road which for a number of years created a split-site operation before the old school was pulled down in 1970 to create a car park. All that remains is the headmaster's study to the far left.

The corner of Roebuck Road and St Margaret's Street looking east, before 1880. The houses, a mixture of rough brick and weatherboard, are typical of the area and period but are in some need of repair especially to the tiles and ground level brickwork. The occupants at the time were James Tullet and next door Alfred Snelling, a shopkeeper, although it is not certain that he traded from this house. To the left is Roebuck Court containing a further seven private houses. The area was rebuilt as Cleveden Terrace in 1880 with the near end called Jersey Terrace and the far end Watts Terrace. The brick pillars of the Roebuck Court gap still remain. The Roebuck public house, estblished in 1787, is behind the camera.

Chatham Central station was rather a misnomer, as it was neither in Chatham nor was it central: the station was a result of intense rivalry between railway companies in the mid-nineteenth century (see also p. 17). The South Eastern Railway had linked London to Strood by 1849 and the East Kent Railway (later London, Chatham and Dover Railway) linked East Kent to Chatham by 1858, ferrying passengers for London to Strood station via a horse bus. Later, the LCDR extended its line to London Victoria leaving the SER stranded at Strood. The SER then built another line crossing the Medway eastwards to stations at Rochester Common and Chatham Central which opened in March 1892; the line was on a viaduct as the LCDR had built a goods yard in the path merely to obstruct progress. The station itself was north of Rochester High Street, parallel to the

railway viaduct to Chatham. The duplication of lines and stations was a drain on both companies so they merged in 1899 making Chatham Central redundant. It lingered until closure on 1 October 1911. For many years the site was derelict with only light industrial units or small warehouses, before being completely cleared recently for a car park.

The lack of tram lines and the gap in the High Street next to the white house (later filled by the new post office in 1913) date the card to around 1902. The public house to the right is the original Star Hotel, demolished in 1926, when the corner was widened into the lower High Street and Corporation Street. The end shop in the High Street was Smetham and Tutt pawnbrokers at 177-179, then came Joseph Hewitt (chemist), Carter Owen (wines and spirits) and Miss Fearnley (milliner) before the gap and then Smith's florist. Opposite, on the corner of Victoria Street, was Lane & Son, a supplier of artists' materials. Even more road widening is now in evidence with the end property now being no. 175 (a butcher's) next to a camera shop, gift shop and estate agent's before the (now closed) post office. Opposite is now Barclays Bank and a new Star Inn has been built just out of view to the right, up the hill.

A very early view of the eastern end of St Margaret's Bank in Rochester High Street, *c.* 1885. The sign over the lane (which later became Bingley Street) advertises J. Terry's greengrocers, who had a shop in King Street. Although the building next door advertises Chambers, a french polisher, Kelly's Directory does not show this to be the actual premises, although Alfred Trembeth Chambers is shown as a shopkeeper in St Margaret's Bank. Later, the building was a post office owned by J Hunnisett. On a sign in front the name is indistinct but the occupation is shown as blind maker. The gable end is covered by advertisements including one for a rehearsal, the *Daily News* and a boot manufacturer. Further along, the spire is likely to be that of the Wesleyan chapel

in the High Street. Over a century on, the current view shows the wall and railings virtually unchanged. The imposing building on the corner is that of J. Knight & Son who have provided a great number of the tugs seen in the port of Rochester since the 1930s.

The Girls' Grammar School was founded on 3 April 1886 with an educational grant of £6,000 from the Wardens and Commonality of Rochester Bridge. The mayoress of Rochester (Mrs Eliza Wingent) laid the foundation stone on 19 May 1888 and the school was opened by the Countess

of Darnley on 22 January 1889. It comprised ten classrooms, a large assembly hall, dining room, lecture, music and art rooms, library, cloakroom, kitchen and a well-stocked laboratory. Conversion of the Mission Hall, Longley Road, added three more classrooms in 1920. There was also a considerable playground and a six-acre playing field. Situated on the corner of Maidstone Road and Longley Road, at the time of the 1905 postcard it had 350 pupils and the headmistress was Miss Dora Sandford MA. Increasing attendance necessitated the building of a new school at the upper end of Maidstone Road. After many years of split-site education the old school was demolished for housing in recent years. The new picture shows part of the current school which is still undergoing extension and improvements.

A postcard of 1918 showing the view eastwards along New Road from the top of Star Hill. New Road was built following a petition from the local population in 1769 for a new route to Chatham; the old route, the High Street, was prone to congestion, poor lighting and disastrous fires. £10,000 was borrowed for the construction, which was paid back using monies raised from toll-gates in Strood (Angel Corner) and Chatham (Hoggs Lane). Chatham had refused to co-operate initially with Strood and Rochester, but on discovering that the New Road, opened in 1772, was taking traffic away from Chatham streets, decided to contribute to its upkeep. Faced by open fields and with a commanding view of the river Medway it soon attracted the local gentry and large private houses were built for professional men and

women. The nearest house to the camera is no. 3 (New Road House), owned by Revd John Bailey, chaplain to St Barts Hospital; no. 13 was the Kent County Hospital for TB. Nowadays New Road House is Rochester Tutors' Independent College and the remaining buildings are mostly private, save the Medway Manor Hotel at nos 12-17.

MILITARY ROAD.

L. C. & D. STATION.

TOWN HALL.

Chatham.

Chapter 3
CHATHAM

A multi-view postcard posted on 20 October 1914 showing the Military Road, the Town Hall, Chatham Station, Victoria Gardens and the Dockyard Gate. The writer of the card, W.B., states: 'There is only one thing that reminds us down here about the war and that is the flying machines and search lights going at night. I have the first wounded man to see yet.'

The land on which Victoria Gardens were created was originally owned by the War Department and was used as a defensive site against a possible Napoleonic War attack on the dockyard. Chatham Corporation first leased and then bought the area and opened it as a public garden to mark Queen Victoria's Diamond Jubilee in 1897. Landscaped with grass, ornamental gardens, bushes and trees, it quickly became a popular area for strolling, sitting on the numerous benches and admiring the view over the River Medway. A bandstand was added hosting twice-weekly concerts in summer and an open-air service was held each Armistice Day. The cannons in front of the flagpole were captured during the Boer War and presented to Chatham. Nowadays few people merely sit there, but it is used as

a short cut to Chatham centre for local schoolchildren and for impromptu games of football, now that the gardens and bushes have disappeared along with the benches, flagpole and cannon.

Looking north down Railway Street to the Town Hall in 1928, the left is dominated by the bulk of the church of St John the Divine, erected in 1821 at a cost of £16,000 provided by the Parliamentary Commissioners for new church buildings. It was constructed in Grecian Doric style, containing ornate carvings, and can accommodate a thousand people. It was improved in 1859 at a further cost of £3,000. The tram, from either the cemetery or the station, continued to Brompton, passing the shops in Railway Street and beyond the cross-roads those in Military Road, stopping at the Town Hall in the distance. On the right are private houses belonging mainly to the professional classes: solicitors, physicians and surgeons. Now the route is crossed by the ring road and the lower part as far as the Town Hall (completely obscured by the Pentagon Centre) has been pedestrianized. Many buildings have disappeared but as the photographs were both taken at the same time of day, the shadows cast by the buildings on the right, now a more eclectic mix, make an interesting comparison.

A turn of the century view shows the south side of the High Street, looking east from the Rochester end. At 16 is Nelson & Co., a domestic machinery depot as the window states: 'suppliers of sewing machines, mangles and wringers, bassinets and mail carts'. At 18 is Henry West, draper, at 20 Richard Pittman, outfitter, at 22 a solicitors and clerk to the Medway Union and Assistance Committee, at 24 Thomas Howe, a photographer, at 26 Fred Clark and at 28 John Highley, a watchmaker. On the corner are the offices of the *Chatham, Rochester and Gillingham News*. After Gundulph Road is the piano warehouse of Godfrey & Co. Ltd. Today there has been little change to the façades of the buildings but their use is now given over to a

Private Shop at 18, Petcare at 20 and Sabre Cleaning at 22. Apart from Tang's Chinese Restaurant at 26, the remaining shops are either empty or closed.

HIGH STREET, CHATHAM.

A postcard of the mid 1920s shows the Sun Hotel canopy on the corner of Medway Street, then the Refuge Assurance and London Joint City Midland Bank. Further along are the Strood Motor Company offices,

W.H. Smith and the Kings Head public house. Tyres are just visible outside Halfords at 101, and beyond that is the solid building owned by Rigo Clothiers. The taller building immediately beyond is Barnard's New Palace of Varieties (see chapter 6, Medway at Leisure). Beyond, the road curves round to the Military Road crossroads. On the right are Murdoch's music and piano store, HS (Home Supply) footwear and the Domestic Bazaar, and at 94-96 Bates' drapers. The junction has since been widened, the Sun Hotel demolished and the bank has become Newcombe's tailors. Further on is a recruitment agency and ski shop. On the right is the Medway Cycle Centre, then two empty properties.

The Palace of Varieties can still be seen on this postcard of 1916, slightly further on from the previous view. On the immediate left is Porter & Co., bootmakers, the N is of Edwin Smith, grocer, then comes George Rosenberg, tailor, before the Palace of Varieties. The awning is Ralph Martin's tobacconists, then beyond are the Scriven dining rooms, the Bull Inn, American Tailoring Co. and Fanbury's Costumiers. Just visible is the Globe Hotel. On the right is the Theatre Royal, also owned by the Barnard family, opened on 31 July 1899 at a cost of £30,000. It could hold an audience of up to 3,000 for London musicals, comedies and opera, and had the largest stage in Kent. The Barnards sold it in 1937 and it became the Royal and Hippodrome, extending the entertainment to include ballet, boxing, pantomime and ice extravaganzas. It suffered from competition from local

cinemas and closed on 20 May 1955. After a long period of neglect while the foyer was used as a shop, there are now plans to restore it to its former glory. Beyond are the Geisha Tea Room and Lloyds Bank, now both empty. Back on the left, the shops are Alan Hill's photographic studios, an empty shop and Estelle, a florist.

Looking west at the junction of Military Road and Railway Street with the High Street. The 1908 picture shows a scene of bustling activity. The London and Counties Bank, established in 1834, is on the corner and was under the charge of manager Henry Holford May. Beyond is the Maypole dairy. The public house on the right is the Horseshoe, so named after the shape of its public bar; next is the Cash Boot Company. Later the junction would require the service of a policeman to control traffic, but now the whole area has been pedestrianized. The bank is now Lloyds with the Halifax Building Society opposite occupying the premises used in the past by Burton's tailors. The modern metal towers contain plaques of local scenes and military history and were erected as part of heritage improvements in 1993.

The view of the Town Hall and Military Road dates from 1910. Sheep graze on The Paddock to the left. The Town Hall was built of Portland and Bath stone, cost £20,000 and was opened by Lord Rosebery in January 1900. The shops in Military Road served the local forces and dockyard and from no. 15 (next to the Constitutional Club, q.v.) are Ive and Lowe (stationers), Robert Martin (naval outfitters), Charles Carvell (bird dealer), Richard Wade (naval and general outfitter), a hairdresser, two more outfitters, an eating house and finally Mrs King's fried fish shop. At the turn of the century this area was also a notorious red-light district. The cart belongs to the New Brompton Co-op Society and is delivering bread. Now The Paddock is gardens, the Town Hall is the Medway Arts Centre and all the shops were swept

away in the early 1970s for the bus station and the dominating Mountbatten House office block, incorporating the Pentagon shopping centre. Much of the area has now (supposedly) been pedestrianized.

These pictures show the site of the house in which the Medway Towns most famous resident, Charles Dickens, lived from 1821 to 1823, between the ages of nine and eleven. It was at St Mary's Place, 18 The Brook. He had moved here from a grander house in

Ordnance Terrace when his father ran into financial difficulties. At that time The Brook was in a poor area, whose eponymous stream was used as an open sewer. Dickens himself attended Mr Giles' school in Clover Lane. The old picture is from the late nineteenth century, when no. 18 was owned by George Ware and offered 'Accommodation for Travellers'. Next door to the right is reputedly the Salvation Army Hall and in between is a property owned by Robert Nash. However, Kelly's Directory of the period shows St Mary's Place being situated where the Town Hall now is. The house itself was pulled down in 1943 and in the late 1960s and early 1970s the whole area was cleared away to build car parks for the Pentagon Centre and a bus station whose access ramp dominates the new picture.

Queen Street in the early years of the twentieth century, looking down from Cross Street to The Brook. Residential buildings typical of the time are undergoing renovation. On the right, the upper properties, before the gap of Randalls Court were owned by James Hooper and George Ellis. The upper left house was owned by Mrs Shannon and both Hill Court and Rose Cottages led off to the side. Nowadays the area is much improved, the street has been widened and all the properties have been completely rebuilt. The provision of handrails for aid in inclement weather is a great help. On the left only no. 8 remains; the rest is given over to a car park. On the right there are six houses rebuilt in the late 1940s or early 1950s.

No book on the Medway Towns would be complete without reference to the Royal Navy which dominated employment and much of the day-to-day life throughout the nineteenth and early twentieth centuries. In 1900, for instance, the Dockyard alone employed 10,000 people. The old view (part of a large series of postcards produced immediately before World War I) shows the barracks parade ground from the terrace. Construction of the new naval barracks was started in May 1897 and they opened in 1903, costing £425,000. The complex was built on the site of Chatham Convict Prison and became home to 4,600 men who had previously been accommodated on warship hulks in the Medway, one of which HMS *Pembroke* gave its name to the barracks. The shadows indicate a post-lunch stroll, which will shortly necessitate the activity of a tidy-up team serving minor punishments to clear up the ground, mostly of cigarette ends. The loss of the Royal Navy from Chatham ended hundreds of years of tradition and the dockyard is now being redeveloped as a heritage area and private housing. The barracks have been taken over by the University of Greenwich's Medway University Campus. The drill hall itself is empty and the parade ground has become an overflow car park for visitors. Naval connections remain in the names of student accommodation blocks: Pembroke, Blake, Nelson, Anson, Grenville and Hawke.

Looking west from beyond the junction with Military Road in 1934: it must be a Sunday as there are no shoppers even though it is around 2 p.m. On the left is Lennard's shoes at 164, Circe Libraries at 162, A.J. Simmons' bakery, then the Freeman, Hardy and Willis shoe emporium. On the right the Boots sign indicates their shop at 149/151, then approaching the camera are: H. Goss (pork butcher), Maypole dairy, Banks and Bryan (mantle warehouse), Jerome Ltd (photographer), Montague Burton (tailor), the Duchess of Edinburgh public house, Goss (again), then Marks and Spencers, in a bazaar with the LNER district agent and the Chatham Billiard Hall sublet on the same site. Military Road is still a thriving

shopping area today. Marks and Spencer have expanded and moved across the street, their old place being taken by JJB Sports. The junction can still be seen just beyond the NatWest Bank on the left.

This old photograph is reputed to be of Whittaker Street in the latter days of the nineteenth century, when it was a typical Chatham street of weatherboarded houses. Whittaker Street dates from the late eighteenth century and once ran from the High Street/Church Street junction to New Road and was in the most part quite steep. The rear of the houses shows the machinery necessary for a washing day, with the sturdy mangles protected from the elements. The street is now considerably foreshortened by the inner ring road. The shops that have replaced private houses in the lower part of the street include a dry cleaners – an appropriate modern counterpart to the old mangles.

The photograph of the upper High Street near Luton Arches is dated 1910 but seems to show a much earlier scene. At least the shops that supposedly stood either side, according to Kelly's Directory of 1910, cannot be identified in the picture. However, as a John Howland had the tenancy of the British Queen pub around the turn of the century it is possible that he is pictured outside. The weatherboarded shop next door seems to be displaying fruit and vegetables but to the extreme right is clearly J.W. Curd's furniture store. The properties further towards Luton are not immediately recognizable as shops at all, despite the existence in the 1910 directory of a stationers here. The street has now been considerably widened but among all the changes the British Queen remains and the ground floor windows

seem reassuringly similar. Much has been rebuilt and the local shops are now Starquest Theatrical Agency, a confectioners and some restaurants or takeaways.

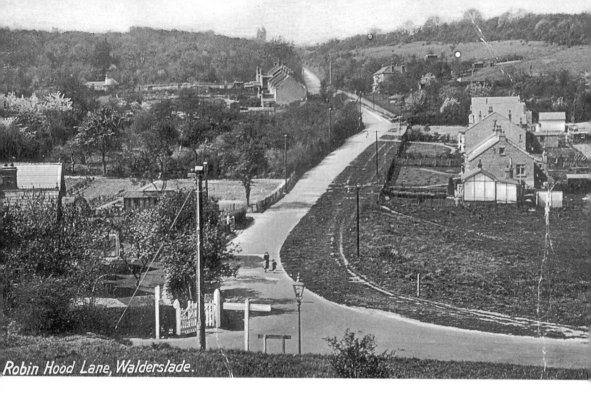

Robin Hood Lane, Walderslade.

In the 1930s Walderslade was just beginning to develop, with small plots of land being sold for development in the existing fields, farmland and orchards. A number of owners joined together as early co-operatives to lend particular skills. One of the earliest houses in this area was Varney House built by a Mr Reeve in 1900 and shown isolated to the right near the top of the picture. On the south side, to the left, the first property was Woodbine Cottage owned by William Slattery, a builder, then Polyfield Cottage, the terrace of Robin Hood Cottages (built in 1906), Fairview and Hillcroft, the home of poultry farmer Thomas Mackintosh. On the right the cottages were named The Nest, Bankview, Sunnyside, Boaz and Devona. In the foreground Boxley Road goes off to the left and the road to Walderslade village itself to the right. Robin Hood Cottages and Hillview remain, though more modern properties such as the Sherwood Oak public house (left) and the BP garage (right) dominate.

A postcard from 1909 showing Gillingham High Street looking eastwards from Canterbury Street. The High Street was originally called Wellington Place and was situated between Marlborough Street and Canterbury Street in what was then New Brompton. Later the name High Street was given to the complete stretch as far as the railway station. Initially the shops were converted terraced houses run by retired dockyard workers or their wives. By the time of the card it was a thriving and substantially built-up area. On the corner is the London and Provincial Bank, then William Miller (tobacconist) and Edward Crawley (estate agent). The smaller of the imposing buildings housed Alfred Rider, corn merchants and family miller.

The large building housed Thomas Dawes & Sons (monumental mason), George Nicholls (grocer) and Horace Bines (plumber). A carving on the façade still reads 'Established 1877. AD 1904 Carrara Buildings'. The building is possibly named after a prime source of marble.

HIGH STREET

Brompton was a village until the eighteenth century when it grew to house the dockyard workers and military men stationed in the nearby barracks. By 1838 it had been recognized as an urban area in its own right. The old picture was taken in 1858 looking down Wood Street towards Dock Road. The large sign is advertising the Duke of Wellington public house run by William Smith; beyond are private houses owned by Sergeant Major Taylor and a Mrs Stokes, among others. The High Street cuts across Wood Street to the right, ending at Brompton Barracks Gate. The pub on the corner is the Crown and the line of houses later became known as Strowse's Buildings after an ironmonger moved into what had been the Crown. It is now Lennox Row. All the houses above it have been demolished but some of the original residential Wood Street remains nearer the new roundabout in Dock Road and Admiralty Terrace.

The photograph of 1913 shows Brompton High Street from the north of Middle Street to Wood Street. At one time it was claimed that Brompton had the most public houses per head of population in Britain. Although the shop on the corner says Swanston, Kelly's notes it as Mrs Lucy Tuffley's dining rooms. Next is John Mehigan (bootmaker), W. Stevens (pork butcher), Hardy Coppin (china/glass), Irene West (confectioners), John Allen (hairdresser), H. Davis (athletic outfitters), the Central Hotel and finally a branch of Smetham and Tutt (pawnbrokers). Now all the shops are gone and flats replaced them in the 1980s. The roads have been widened if only for parking but the bulk of Brompton Barracks is clearly visible at what was the original end of the High Street.

The main entrance of what was then the Royal Naval Hospital in 1931. It was opened by King Edward VII on 26 July 1905 on Windmill Hill, Gillingham, replacing the smaller, obsolete Melville Hospital close to the Dockyard Gate. Covering 29 acres, it cost £800,000 and could accommodate 500 patients. It was built of red brick and Doulton stone and a major feature was a corridor of 1,000 feet linking all the main wards. A separate outbuilding housed an isolation ward for sufferers of contagious diseases. It had in total nine medical officers, seven sisters and seventy sick-berth ratings and was known for its high quality of medical care in the days before the NHS. When the Royal Navy left the Medway Towns in 1959, the hospital was given over to the NHS, which provided £1 million to modernize it as the Medway Hospital. Four new operating theatres were created along with enhanced facilities for geriatrics and mental illness patients. Much of the original façades remain, however, as does the clock tower which has become the hospital logo. See also chapter 5, Medway at Work.

The Grand Cinema was opened in December 1910 as a variety theatre that occasionally showed films. Owned by H. Barr and situated on the corner of Skinner Street and Jeffrey Street, it had 800 tip-up seats, a large screen and high, ornate ceilings. Films alternated with the usual variety acts until 4 April 1914 when it re-opened as purely a cinema; it was taken over by the Schieffers in 1915. The picture dates from around 1930 and shows the cinema in its heyday before it fell victim to the decline of British cinemas in the 1950s when many alternative forms of entertainment became widely available. It finally closed on 12 November 1960 and was pulled down in 1965. The site is now occupied by the Kwik-Fit car park and Kent Custom Bike Shop, although a link to the past is retained in the name Grand Court on flats just out of the picture to the left.

High Street, Gillingham

A 1915 postcard of the High Street looking west from Canterbury Street corner, showing a busy shopping area. The Prince Albert pub on the right was run by Mrs E. Morgan, next door was Edwards and Gittings (tailors), then Eastman's (butchers), Fred Bloor (curiosities and toys), Mrs Bloor (costumier), William Moss (greengrocer) and J. Haylock (boots). On the left were William Parkins (watchmaker), Bert Bullock (tailor), Harry Baker (butcher), Miss Cunningham (fancy repository), Arthur Carey (corn and flour merchant) and the Medway farm and dairy. This area was the original High Street, before expansion eastwards to the station. The street is now pedestrianized but remains a busy shopping area; the Prince Albert remains, followed by a charity shop, a grocers called I Can't Believe It, and the Eel Pie Island Café. The left-hand parade contains a card shop, thrift shops, a greengrocers and a newsagents.

By 1924, Gillingham High Street was showing signs of expansion and progress, attracting a number of prestigious shops as seen in this postcard. On the immediate left are Charles Connelly (greengrocer), Curry's Ltd (cycle manufacturer), then Treadwell's (bootmakers). On the corner of James Street, a butcher and tobacconist come before the twin-turreted Congregational church, built in 1869 when the street was purely residential. Just beyond at 120 stands Woolworths, then the Conservative Club on the corner of Gardiner Street. The large three-storey building with the clock is the Co-operative Society and Assembly Hall. Now, the same mix of large and small is visible although the street is now pedestrianized. Woolworths remains on the same site, Littlewoods occupies the church site and the Co-op

was demolished in 1978 to be replaced by Clarks shoe shop and W.H. Smith. Gardiner Street is now Sappers' Walk, a name which recognizes the contribution of the Royal Engineers to Gillingham.

A view of 1904 looking west down the High Street from the railway station forecourt. The Railway Hotel at 170 was first mentioned in 1860 and changed its name to the Southern Belle in 1979. The landlord in 1904 was John T. Winter. Next door is Henry Tremain (greengrocer), then the ornate frontage of Arthur Stookes' chemists, H.C.G. Kirby (stationers), George Hicks (butchers) and Mrs Hollings, beer retailer at 158. By 1904 the Britannia public house is shown at this number the present day sign states 'Established 1856'. Further down at 136-142 was the magnificently named New Brompton Economical Industrial and Provident Society Ltd, a forerunner of the Co-op which remains on the same site. The bay window of the chemists remains but is now part of a café, the upper brickwork being lost. The other shops are mainly cafés and butchers.

Ye Old Five Bells is one of the oldest public houses in Gillingham. It was built in 1700 on the site of what was reputedly the oldest house in Gillingham. It is situated in Church Street facing the Green and in the middle of the original parish of Gillingham. Its name is derived from the number of bells at St Mary's parish church at the time. It has also been called the Five Bells and Cricketers and Five Bells and Cricket Player Inn, which refer to the times when cricket was played on the Green. At one time, meetings of the Manorial and Court Leet were held there, which upheld the law in the area, levied taxes and fines for such offences as 'running unlicensed alehouses' or 'throwing dung'. Nowadays the view is little changed, except for the parked cars and the gasometer by the Strand.

The Jezreelites were a religious sect founded by a local soldier, James White of the 16th Foot, who changed his name to James Jershom Jezreel. Being disillusioned with conventional religion, the sect was based on Christian Israelites, believing that they would be saved in the 'final gathering of AD 2000'. They followed a form of communal living, with White controlling the finances and opening shops in the sect's name. Much money was ploughed into building a tower to Heaven which began in 1884. Despite claiming immortality, Jezreel died in 1885 and his successor, widow Esther, in 1888. The sect fell to infighting with claims of financial irregularities and split up. The tower remained incomplete as funds diminished, but was only pulled down in 1961 all the other sect properties were sold off. The postcard of 1906 shows the unfinished tower from Watling Street, the panels containing religious carvings. Now the site is occupied by a Jubilee Clip factory.

The corner of Canterbury Street and Rainham Road looking east in 1909, showing the tramlines passing alongside Victorian residential houses. Further along was a designated tram lane where the maximum speed could be achieved. At the time the area was known as Jezreel Corner. The shop on the corner is that of S. & E. Lingley, dyers and cleaners, with the receiving office of the Clarence Sanitary Laundry. Next door is William Grist, tobacconist and confectioner. The rest of the houses to beyond Chester Road and Park Avenue to the left are private. At no. 18 were the offices of Taunton and Low, physicians and surgeons. Now the corner shop is Mellor's newsagents followed by the A2 hairdressers. The houses beyond remain private.

65

RAINHAM MARK, KENT.

Rainham Mark originally denoted the line between Gillingham and Rainham; the name comes from the Old English *mearc,* meaning a boundary. By the time of the 1930s card, Rainham had been joined administratively to Gillingham. It is reputedly the place where Henry VIII first met his fourth wife, Anne of Cleves. On the corner is George Earnest Burley, butchers. The gable end is advertising new local homes. Further shops are a confectioner's and general store before R.G. Hodges (motor engineers), Stephen Harrison (newsagent and post office), further private houses, another general store and finally Rainham Mark Social Club. Now much is gone, the lone Austin Seven replaced by non-stop trunk road traffic. The end shop is now Sophisticuts hairstylist, followed by a Shell petrol station, the Rainham Mark newsagents, off-licence and post office and the Hop and Vine public house (previously the Belisha Beacon).

The National School was opened in 1846 on the corner of Station Road and the High Street. The curate, Reverend F.F. Haslewood, raised the cost – £685 – from local subscriptions, the land being donated by the Earl of Thanet. An infants' school was added in 1866 at a cost of £500 as the original room could not hold all the pupils. At the time of the photograph, around 1920, the school could cater for 600 pupils. Gradually the school became outdated and overcrowded so pupils were transferred to other newly built schools in the area, notably in Solomon Road and Orchard Street. By 1967 only the infants remained and some of the remaining rooms were used by a youth club and as the parish hall, and the old school closed. It was demolished in

1977 to make way for the shopping precinct behind the parade of modern shops, still mostly empty, in the new photograph.

The shops in Station Road, seen here looking north in the late 1920s, started immediately beyond the National School railings. They were typical of the time, serving the many needs of the local community. At no. 1 was W. and R. Fletcher's butchers, then Alf Callaway (pork butchers), Frank Monk (fish), then the Rainham Co-op's meat department, private houses, Fred Fischer (fruiterer) and finally Albert Sutton (grocer) before Langley Road to the left. Nowadays still given over to shops, the mixture of bookmakers, newsagents, cafés, sandwich bars, takeaways, gift shops and the Rainham Bookshop reflects both the changing needs of customers and the removal to shopping precincts of those shops that provided basic day-to-day needs.

The tram service from Chatham Town Hall to Rainham started in August 1906 and was used extensively by Chatham Dockyard employees (who were summoned to departure times by clanging bells) and later by schoolchildren. The card is dated 1909 and the crowds may indicate an occasion or merely curiosity at a photographer. The Cricketers Inn is first mentioned in 1766 and remained as pictured until it was pulled down in the 1930s. It was rebuilt further back from the High Street in the Tudor style seen in the modern picture. Trams needed to stop in the middle of the road to let passengers on and off, which caused considerable congestion, so in 1929 the terminus was moved to Station Road off to the right. A new service was introduced from

Rainham to Strood Hill in 1928 (at the agreed rate of a halfpenny a mile this would have cost 4d). The trams were replaced on 30 September 1930 by a bus service run by the same company, later to become the Maidstone and District.

RAM TERMINUS, RAINHAM, KENT.

The lower, eastern end of Rainham High Street in 1910 shows a mixture of contemporary shops and private houses. On the left was the post office, then Bertram Catt (jewellers), Barclays Bank and Rosina Stopps (draper), before some private houses to Ivy Street. The post office survives *in situ*. Other shops here today are PDQ Secretarial Services then private houses and an accountant's. On the right Hidson's Car Sales have replaced the area previously occupied by Quinnell's hardware and Belmont House, including the area cleared by the demolition of properties before no. 118 (note that the High Street has been renumbered).

This card shows close-up detail of two shops at the end of the High Street before the gap and Scott Avenue, in 1902. At 147 (old numbering) is Tucker's watch repairers and jewellers which stayed in family hands as a jeweller's until 1985 when the last of the family shopkeepers died. Although now a hairdresser's, note that little of the frontage has changed, unlike that of no. 149, Richardson's cycle works trading under the BSA Bicycles sign and also offering sewing machines: this is now the Rainham Newsagents. In the intervening years it also served as a confectioner's. The gap beyond once contained The Russels, a large house owned by the Quinnell family, well-known Rainham shopkeepers (see also p. 70).

Although a village called Wydemere (meaning wide pool) existed in 1270, Wigmore owes its current origins to the expansion of Gillingham southwards in the early years of this century. At the same time there was a decline in the need for agricultural land which was being sold off for £20 an acre. A plot measuring 20 by 200ft could be bought for £10. These proved popular, despite having no amenities (even though mains water came to Wigmore Road itself, then consisting only of shacks and holiday homes, by 1904). Wigmore then was a wooded area with fruit, chicken or pig farms. Expansion was more rapid after 1910, when smallholdings and ready-built bungalows and villas were offered for sale at 275 guineas (£288 15s). Free transport was provided for potential purchasers. The old view, a postcard from around 1920 looking north along Wigmore Road from the Fairview Avenue cross-roads, still shows a semi-rural aspect. By the time of the Second World War there was a thriving community, but the tremendous explosion in house-building, resulting in the current view, took place in the 1950s and after. It is now almost a town in its own right, having extended south to the M2 motorway.

The firm of CAV moved from Acton in London into the works vacated by Short Bros on Rochester Esplanade in 1949. The company had been founded by Charles Anthony Vanderbilt at the turn of the century and specialized in diesel fuel injection pumps. It was typical of engineering works in the Medway area at that time, which apart from the Dockyard itself included Winget's, Elliot's and various companies in the Knight Road area of Strood. This view shows the turning shop where fully skilled turners, having served a five year apprenticeship, manufactured precisely engineered parts (see also p. 78).

Chapter 5

MEDWAY AT
WORK

The work ethic started very early in life then as it does now. The old photograph is of an infants' class in Strood, probably at the turn of the century given the style of the pinafore dresses, collars and sailor suits. The school is unidentified but thought to be in the Wainscott or Frindsbury area. Compare their clothes with the smart turnout of Reception Year Class 5 of Bligh Way Infants' in 1998 under teacher Ms Gilmore and classroom assistant Ms Hubbard. The only point of comparison is possibly some of the children's hairstyles.

In the early part of the century most bulk goods were transported by sailing barge or rail. Smaller loads were carried by horse and cart until the twenties and thirties when lorries became the norm. The old photograph shows local hauliers Fairclough's delivering a considerable load of paper to Mackays printing works in Fair Row, Chatham, in the late 1930s. Nowadays most large concerns have their own transport fleets as illustrated by the Homebase lorry. Note that even the loading and unloading are mechanized.

The old view shows the Borstal village policeman at the turn of the century, outside his house, probably supplied by the police force. He would have been concerned with mainly rural crimes plus a little theft as Borstal then was an isolated village. A PC would have been stationed there more as a public relations exercise and was regarded as a pillar of the community. Armed with an ebony truncheon and shackle handcuffs he patrolled on foot or cycle with help a whistle blow away. Despite being part of the Rochester City Police Force, he would have been autonomous in his area. Nowadays PC Roscoe Walford (in the modern picture) covers the Borstal area as well as the High Street, Delce and Warren Wood as a community officer with a more diverse area, more social issues and transient crimes to contend with. Patrol is by car, more often in pairs, and assistance is provided by a telescopic baton, radio, CS gas and rigid handcuffs. Similarities with the earlier view are the helmets (flat caps are used when driving), the colour of the uniform and the philosophy of 'stop crime rather than solve it'. The spine on the helmet is a traditional throwback to the time when policemen doubled as firemen.

Hops have been grown in Britain as a medicinal herb since around AD 800 and were first used for brewing in the fifteenth century. Hop-picking traditionally brought armies of people from as far away as the Midlands, but they came mainly from London to Kent, both for a holiday and to earn some much-needed ready cash. The Medway hop area was centred on Luton and Rainham. The hops grew on bines tied to poles about 12ft high and were usually picked in September. The bine was cut and pulled down for the pickers to strip hops into a basket or large bin for speedy transportation to an oast house for drying. The lines of pickers were known as drifts. On some farms the poles themselves were pulled down using a hop dog tool and laid across the bins. Women and children worked mainly the weekdays (as shown) and were joined by their menfolk at the weekends. A basket contained six bushels and when full earned 1s in the 1920s. Conditions could also be harsh. Since the late 1950s mechanical harvesting has taken over, whereby a few can process in days the volume of hops that took hundreds of pickers weeks to do in the past. Bines are now cut and transported to mechanical picking sheds where they are strung on conveyors and the hops stripped off into sacks. The residue is returned to the soil.

Another picture of CAV Ltd (see also p. 73). This is the drilling shop in the original Esplanade factory just after the Second World War, when all the drilling was a skilled manual operation. The firm, now known as Lucas Varity Ltd, moved to Hoath Lane, Rainham, in 1970, doubled in size in 1976 and is now the second largest employer in the area, with 2,000 employees. It still offers training and apprenticeships and now makes pumps for the worldwide market; the Medway factory is the world centre of excellence for diesel fuel injection equipment for the Lucas Group. Most operations are now automated, with one man controlling machinery that used to take five people to operate. In drilling (shown here), the

operation is computer-controlled and robot-loaded. A synthetic water-based recyclable coolant is used to disseminate heat from the process.

Although purporting to be Chatham sorting office in 1920, this photograph actually shows the Rochester office, which was situated at the rear of the post office in the High Street. At the time of the old picture all mail in the area covered by Rochester, both outgoing and incoming, would have been sorted here by hand. It was a constant operation, as there were many more deliveries per day than now. It was possible for instance to send a postcard in the morning to arrange an evening meeting the same day, confident in the knowledge that the message would be received in time. Now mail is collected throughout the Medway area and sent to Maidstone where it is sorted for sending onward. Incoming mail is received by sorting offices in Snodland, Rochester and Best Street, Chatham, as shown in this modern picture, where it is sorted into individual rounds using the racks and pigeon holes shown.

Following a tragic house fire in 1901 when assistance from Rochester arrived too late, the local population petitioned for a Cliffe brigade. This was created in 1904, the year of the old photograph, which shows Capt. Robertson (third from the left) and his men in front of their Shand and Mason horse-drawn pump. The station was then in Buttway Road and the horses were stabled round the corner in North Road. The team consisted of the captain, nine firefighters and a driver. The current brigade has been stationed in Church Street since 1963 and are retained firefighters, i.e. some have other occupations but as a front-line team can be called to assist anywhere in the event of a large 'shout'. The Cliffe team were frequent winners of the Glanfield Trophy for pump competitions, the only retained men to

do so. The current team members pictured in front of their Dennis SS139 appliance (with a 500-gallon-a-minute Godiva two-stage pump) are, from the left: Sub Officer Rob Stead, Andy Morrad, Mick Gadd, Malcolm Jones, Wayne Harrison, Nigel Williams and Oliver Mitchell.

The road gang, pictured in around 1880, are repairing or resurfacing part of St Margaret's Street in Rochester with large cobbles called setts. Most of the materials and tools were carried by horse and cart but the final surface was created by the locally manufactured (in Strood) Aveling and Porter road roller. Note the Invicta logo on the block above the front roller, which was conical in shape allowing for the two separate rolls to be close together on the ground while maintaining the ability to adjust to the contour of the roadway. Nowadays road rollers are a rare sight. More common are the multipurpose JCBs and tippers such as those shown here working on the Medway Tunnel link road in Frindsbury.

The river front in Frindsbury is dominated by cement factory chimneys in this picture from 1911, taken from a point near Blue Boar Wharf in Rochester. Cement manufacturing began in 1851 when William Tingley set up a factory using the plentiful local chalk and clay and the nearby river for importing other raw materials and exporting the finished product. The initial works quickly expanded and by the turn of the century the combined factories employed 750 workers and turned out 3,900 tons of cement a week, transported by 200 sailing barges, some of which are also shown here. The works shown, mostly controlled by the Tingleys, are from the left: Phoenix, Globe, Bridge, Crown, Quarry and Beaver. The trade went into recession at the time of the picture and soon only the Crown factory was left, which itself closed in the 1960s. A link is retained in the name of the Phoenix

Industrial Estate, which includes Phoenix Wharf and Crown Wharf. The units are now let to distribution and warehousing concerns like Transit Medway, using jetties such as Laser Quay and Sunderland Quay along with the newly integrated road system leading to the Medway Tunnel.

This 1914 picture shows nurses who are thought to be part of the Voluntary Aid Detachment, set up to look after First World War soldiers convalescing after front-line injuries. Many local houses were requisitioned for this work and annexed to the main hospitals. The one shown is thought to be Cypress House in Frindsbury. The recent photograph shows the nursing and medical staff at the Medway Hospital Accident and Emergency unit (see also p. 58). In the A&E unit (the only one in the Medway Towns), 16 doctors and 50 nurses attend to 200 patients a day (some 75,000 a year) from a catchment area of 350,000. Currently there is a £55 million redevelopment scheme designed to bring all departments on site, including those currently at All Saints' and St Bartholomew's Hospitals, which should be completed during 1999.

The Richman Brothers' removal firm was founded in Gillingham by twins Henry and William in 1880. Originally using only a handcart as general carriers, they quickly progressed to horse-drawn carts and then wagons as shown here in around 1910. It was thought that the Richman horses were trained to find their own way home, allowing the driver a crafty sleep! From depots in Gillingham Road and Beresford Road they gradually expanded their business and included warehousing until by the mid-1980s they owned fourteen removal vans and six trailers and were finding lack of space a problem. Although moving subsequently to Sittingbourne, they have retained offices in Gillingham. Nowadays there are numerous but smaller local removal firms as illustrated

here, as well as many smaller carriers and self-drive firms catering for the changing needs of the local population who, as elsewhere, are now more inclined to do it themselves.

3307 Chatham. Leaving the Dockyard.

No chapter on Medway work would be complete without reference to the largest employer, the Chatham Dockyard, some of whose workers are shown leaving work in this postcard of 1902. The view is along Dock Road from the Wood Street corner, Brompton. At the bottom of the hill on the right would be a long line of trams with the destinations carved onto stone plaques on the wall; they would go as far afield as Maidstone and Sheerness. The plaques have recently been restored. The dockyard was founded by Elizabeth I in 1570 and by the 1880s had expanded considerably, employing 10,000 people in 1900. The rapid growth of the Medway Towns, especially in Brompton, Chatham and Gillingham, is due to the need to house dockyard and other workers involved in trade linked to the military. The dockyard closed in 1984 and most of the buildings were demolished. The eastern portion became a port complex, some buildings were given over to residential and industrial use and the rest was converted into a tourist-orientated historic dockyard. Dock Road itself carries traffic via the new Medway Tunnel from Frindsbury to Chatham.

At the turn of the century one of the major sources of entertainment for the local population was the variety theatre. At that time the Medway Towns had many; the largest and one of the most popular was Barnard's Palace of Varieties at 107 High Street, Chatham. The original Palace of Varieties had been opened by Dan Barnard as a music hall attached to the Railway Tavern in 1850. When this burnt down in 1885 Lou Barnard (Dan's son) built a larger music hall on the same spot, called Barnard's New Palace of Varieties, which staged comedy and dramatic acts. It was subsequently burnt down accidentally on 18 March 1934 and was replaced by shops.

Chapter 6
MEDWAY AT LEISURE

The area known as the Strand is virtually the only local site with a beach used for leisure purposes. Leisure activities here date from 1896, when an open-air swimming pool was opened by Mr Cuckow. Changing rooms converted from railway carriages were added in 1920 along with a chlorine supply and filters. Between the wars the area became very popular (as shown in the 1930 postcard) with the addition of a paddling pool, boating pool, putting green, bandstand and café. By the late 1930s it was attracting up to 12,000 visitors a day. A miniature railway was added in 1948 and swings and roundabouts a year later. From the 1950s attendances dropped as alternative forms of leisure became available. Nowadays activity centres on the covered Strand Leisure Pool and bouncy castle/swing area shown in the distance in the modern picture. A paddling pool remains along with the miniature train and café, but the original paddling/boating area is now an overflow car park.

Proudly displaying their troop flag and winning shields are the 40th Medway Scout Troop of St Mary's church in Frindsbury in 1927. Their leaders were the Revd M. Treacher (vicar), the Revd Preston (curate and scout master) and Mr Barnes (group scout master). The Scout movement was founded in 1907 by Lord Baden Powell, who aimed to encourage the physical, spiritual and mental development of young people so that they might take a constructive place in society. Now the uniform is modernized, though many links with tradition can be seen in the recent photograph of the 21st Strood Scout Troop under Group Scout Leader Roger Spain.

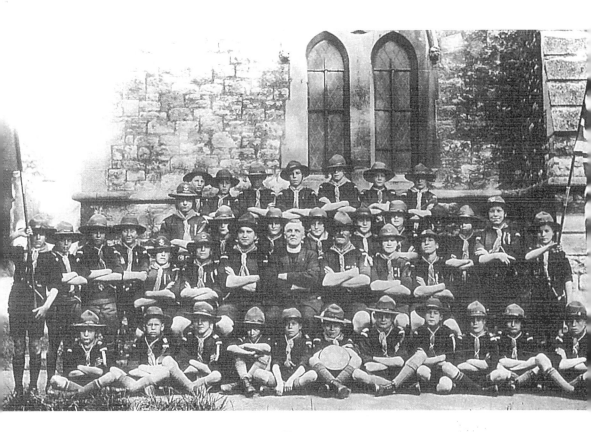

The rather serious and formal group of young men are the Chatham ASE cycling club in 1900. The late Victorian age saw the expansion of leisure and sporting clubs devoted to hiking, swimming, tennis and cycling, both for recreation and socializing. Not only was cycling popular as a sport but for many it was the only form of transport. The Medway Wheelers cycling club was formed in 1929 from a youth club in Luton and soon merged with a Gillingham club. The golden era of cycling was during the 1950s, when the Wheelers were team champions of Great Britain for six years. In 1968 they merged with the Medway Velo cycling club. Wigmore cycling club was formed as an offshoot from a social club in 1950. Both clubs now have roughly fifty members, some of whom are seen pictured to the left at the Harrietsham time trials in 1998.

Given the extensive military (particularly naval) presence in the Medway Towns, it is perhaps not surprising that much leisure time is spent in public houses! These contrasting pictures from 1890 and 1998 both show the White Hart at the west end of Rochester High Street, near the Guildhall. The White Hart is one of the oldest public houses in the Towns, reputedly dating back to 1396, but this may be confused with another public house of the same name. Records are unclear until the first documented reference in 1783 when the landlord was John William. It took its name from the badge of Richard II. Rebuilding was undertaken by the Meux Brewery in 1906 and there were further additions in 1950. Until the late 1960s it was part of a row of shops and private houses between the Guildhall and Rochester Bridge.

It was then rebuilt and left at the end of the row by the bridge conversion and road widening of 1969. It was threatened by a proposed expansion by the Museum to create a collection of Victoriana in 1994 but has now been refurbished and renamed 'Expectations' (another enterprise in Rochester adopting a Dickensian cachet). It nestles beside the Medway Conservancy Offices.

From around 1900 until the late 1950s a trip on a paddle steamer was a popular method of spending spare time. Running from Strood, Sun Pier in Chatham and Upnor Piers to Herne Bay, Sheerness (later Clacton) and Southend, the majority of the steamers were owned by the Medway Steam Packet Company. They afforded a break from industrial and city life, unlimited open air and a trip to the seaside. The

Prince of Wales, shown here approaching Sun Pier in 1910, was built in steel by R. Craggs of Middlesbrough in 1896 and ran on a Medway to Southend service until 1917 when the Admiralty used her (renamed *Padua*) to run the Medway naval ferry service. After being chartered to the Firth of Forth she returned to the Medway and was sold for breaking up to Messrs T. Ward in 1928 at Acorn Wharf, Rochester. The paddle steamer trips ended when the last remaining vessel, the *Medway Queen,* was withdrawn on 8 September 1963. In recent years the service has re-appeared, now undertaken by the *Kingswear Castle,* built in 1924 for the River Dart in Devon and after a period of neglect restored to working order in 1985. Based at Chatham Dockyard (where she is shown here), she offers local cruises and special sailings further afield from the dockyard, Rochester, Sun and Strood Piers. A society is also dedicated to restoring the *Medway Queen.*

As well as cycling clubs, tennis clubs became very popular for social and recreational reasons, mostly for the middle classes, in the late Victorian and early Edwardian eras. The photograph of 1910 is entitled Temple Street Tennis Club, but the exact location remains unidentified. It shows a demonstration of serving, possibly by an official, honoured guest or famous player. Note the high proportion of ladies and the regulation white clothing. The modern photograph, which amply demonstrates the changes in clothing and racquets, is of the Winget and Chatham Luton ladies' teams and other club members. Winget Tennis Club is one of the longest-running clubs in the area; it celebrated its golden anniversary recently and is still based in Strood, although the eponymous factory closed down many years ago.

Just strolling was an easily achieved and cheap form of pleasure in the late Victorian age. The Castle Gardens and the Vines attracted great numbers of walkers in Rochester. The postcard of the Vines shows the avenue of plane trees quite mature but still in protective ironwork: this dates it to around 1910. The Vines was once the monks' vineyard attached to the Priory of St Andrew. In 1880 the Corporation of Rochester leased it from the Dean and Chapter and laid it out as a public park. It is bounded by Crow Lane (formerly Maidstone Road), Vines Lane and the Kings School. The present-day comparison shows some of the trees which survived the hurricane of October 1987, as well as some of the saplings planted to replace those felled. On the left is 'The Monk' by Robert Koenig, carved from a 100-year-old plane tree and unveiled on 9 July 1997.

The Invicta cinema in Strood was opened on 3 November 1919 by H.G. and W. Croneen, who also owned Invicta cinemas in Chatham and Gillingham. They also later built the Plaza in Gillingham. The Strood Invicta saw considerable trade in the heyday of the cinema during the 1930s (as in this photograph) until bomb damage caused its temporary closure in 1945. After the war it reopened as the Wardona and was known for its Saturday morning children's matinées in the 1950s until its closure in 1959. The site is now occupied by Kwiksave. Strood acquired its own cinema again in 1996 with the building of the Virgin Multiplex close to the M2 bridge off Cuxton Road. The cinema has nine screens, including a première screen,

a café bar and a video and book shop and is part of an entertainment complex of sports clubs, night clubs and restaurants.

The Chatham Public Library and Museum was one of many set up around the start of the twentieth century to benefit the local communities. It was sited at the lower end of New Road close to the Luton Arches area. It was made possible by a bequest of £4,500 from the philanthropist Andrew Carnegie which left the Corporation with only £500 to find. It opened in October 1903 with 12,000 books and manuscripts on two floors. In the early days it appeared that access was almost by appointment only. By the late 1960s the library had added a reference section, junior library, photocopier, music scores, records and pictures, all as a public service. Branch and mobile library services were also available. The library was moved to Riverside Gardens in the 1970s and the old building was demolished. The current picture shows the lighter and airier layout of a modern Medway library, with further information only a keyboard away: this one is at Strood.